MAKE YOUR BANKER HAPPY

**10 Keys to Unlocking
a Good Relationship with Your Banker**

MAKE YOUR BANKER HAPPY

GARY FURR

Business
Success
Publishing

ISBN 9781091201422

TABLE OF CONTENTS

THROUGH GOOD TIMES AND BAD

Many business leaders attribute the success of their business to an innovative idea, hard work, and the right talent, and those are critical factors. One factor that is often underestimated is the role bankers play. When I was general manager and chief operations officer of a $40 million company with seven locations, I was responsible for the finance department as well as all other departments. One of the things I learned in finance is that you have to have a good relationship with your banker.

Our banker was essential to our success since business does not always go as planned. There were times when business dropped off and the relationship we had established with our banker kept us going. Since the relationship was long-term, they understood our business cycles and worked with us during tough times.

I speak with a lot of business owners and few ever tell me that they have a solid, ongoing relationship with their banker. Under those circumstances, my advice is always the same: You need to get to know your banker—now. Establish that relationship in good times because when bad times come, as they always do, you will have that trusting relationship in place.

To help the people I work with establish those relationships, I decided to go to the bankers themselves and find out what they are looking for in their customers.

I surveyed ten established bankers in the Portland, Oregon metropolitan area. These are bankers that typically work with small to mid-market businesses. The individual banker's years in banking ranged from fourteen to almost forty years, with the average being twenty-four years. These are seasoned business bankers with a lot of business experience.

The sweet spot (where most of the customers are) for the bankers were businesses in the $5 million to $30 million range, and with two bankers working with clients up to $100 million in revenue and one working with clients with up to $75 million in revenue. However, all of the bankers are more than willing to work with smaller companies with good financials and business practices. Every one of the bankers interviewed likes working with companies with good values that are focused on making money and growing their businesses.

Based on the questions I asked, the responses fell into ten key areas that are part of establishing a solid, trusting relationship:

1. Financials
2. Credit
3. Communication
4. Business practices
5. Management team
6. Professionalism
7. Customer focus
8. Appreciation of the relationship
9. Being proactive
10. Succession plans

Their suggestions and guidance provide a blueprint for establishing the kind of banking relationship that will serve you and your business. 💲

FOCUS ON FINANCIALS

All of the bankers I interviewed said that their best customers are focused on their financials on a regular basis and provide accurate information when asked. No surprise here since the numbers drive everything in your business and if you are not focused on the numbers, then you do not know if your business is winning or losing the game.

Not knowing your financials is like going to a sporting event and not being able to see the scoreboard. You think your team is winning but you are not sure because you cannot see the scoreboard. The scoreboards in your business are your financials: the P&L (profit & loss) statement, balance sheet, and cash flow projection.

The bankers I interviewed want their customers to understand and be focused on their financials, and to provide accurate information and realistic projections to the bank in a timely manner. This requires you, the business owner, to have a deep understanding of your financials and to be reviewing them often. This is not achieved by managing your business from your checkbook and spreadsheets, but by actively reviewing and comparing your P&L statement, balance sheet, and cash flow on a minimum of a monthly basis and preferably weekly.

Bankers like businesses that produce a budget and then compare their actual to the original budget on a regular basis. This is how you track how you are doing in your business on an ongoing basis; there is no good reason to wait until the end of the year for surprises, and bankers do not want to see that either. Producing a budget and comparing it to actual is how you measure performance. The good news is that which we measure tends to improve.

I find that far too often business owners are not paying close attention to their financials; instead they wait until the end of the year to see how they are doing. I have had business owners tell me they know where they are even though they are not paying attention to their financials. When I ask how that is possible they say, "I have money in my checking account so I know how I am doing." That is not how you get your banker to love you. Your banker does not want to see your checkbook register or your spreadsheets; your banker wants to see your financial statements generated by an accounting software package.

When I asked the bankers what percentage of their customers know and understand their numbers, most said 25 to 50 percent. Obviously there is work to be done. A few of the bankers said that 50 to 100 percent of their clients know their numbers, and these are their very best clients. If you are not in the 50 to 100 percent that understand their numbers, it is time to change.

The bankers I interviewed said that their best customers know their numbers and provide the information in a timely manner; saying their very best customers provide the information before even being asked. What I found particularly interesting—and telling—is that the bankers who discussed their very best customers have trimmed their client list down to only the very best businesses, where the business owner knows and understands their financials and often communicates with the bank before being asked. The bankers who responded that 50–100 percent of their clients understand their numbers were also bankers who said they have weeded out the poor-performing clients and are only dealing with clients that understand their numbers and perform well. They no longer will work with clients who do not understand their financials, or have poor business practices and/or poor performance.

Not surprisingly, the bankers report that their most challenging customers do the opposite of what their best customers do—which is pay attention and understand their financials. Considering that the greatest cause of poor performance is not knowing your numbers, it is time to get serious about understanding your financials. You are the business owner; if you do not understand or pay attention to your financials and are unable to provide accurate reports in a timely manner, this will send a big red flag to your banker (and it causes them to want even more information). If you are solely depending on your bookkeeper or CPA to provide you the numbers without you reviewing them for accuracy and understanding them, you are putting your business at risk. I have seen far too many bookkeepers and CPAs who just fill in the blanks and are not providing their customers with guidance.

Again, the numbers drive everything in your business. You do not need to be an accountant or have an accounting degree, but you do need some basic accounting knowledge. Doing business without understanding your numbers is a bit like driving a car without instruments. You may think you are going 70 mph when you are only doing 35 mph. Or you thought you had a full tank of gas, but it was really only one quarter full.

Just like a musician needs to understand the language of music—sharps, flats, chords, and so forth—you need to understand the language of business, which is accounting. As your business grows, you can no longer manage the business from your checkbook. Keeping clear and accurate records for your business is critical to your success.

Most of the bankers I interviewed said that they do not require a cash flow projection, despite the fact that your cash flow statement is an important internal tool to track the movement of cash in and out of your business. Some bankers said not enough businesses produce them, and others said that very few companies below $5 million in revenue generate cash flow projections. While they agreed that business owners should be producing them, they do not require them.

(Note: The Small Business Administration (SBA) does require cash flow projections.) However, the bankers also stated that the well-run companies they work with understand their cash flow.

If you want your banker to love you, make sure you provide him or her with regular and accurate financial statements, such as your monthly and YTD P&L statement as well as the P&L comparison to the same period of time for the previous year or two. Provide an accurate balance sheet and a rolling six-month cash flow projection as well as a budget. Many of the lenders do not require the cash flow projection, but I highly recommend that you not only understand the cash flow but you also provide a copy to your banker. Too many business owners only pay attention to their P&L and net income; those who fall into that trap often do not understand that net income is the theory of cash, not actually cash, since the P&L only takes into account revenue and expense items but does not take into account debt payments, owners' draws, disbursements, or dividends.

Make sure you have reviewed your financials for accuracy before providing them to the bank. I had a client who showed up for a meeting with his banker with financials in hand, not realizing that instead of accrual accounting his bookkeeper had printed them in cash-based accounting. The statements are not the same and banks prefer accrual accounting principles. Missteps like this can be embarrassing, but they can also raise red flags for your banker. Let us take a closer look at the information your banker needs.

Profit and Loss Statement or Income Statement

The P&L (profit & loss) or income statements are simply a report of your revenue minus your expenses, which equals profit. Your P&L should be prepared and reviewed no less than monthly. Far too many business owners wait until the end of the year to see if they made money or not. Income statements are like a movie of a period of time in your business; for example, quarter one (Q1), quarter two (Q2), or YTD. It is important to note that the P&L and balance sheet are lagging indicators, and when you get them from your accountant or bookkeeper, the information may be three or four weeks old. Know and understand where you are and be prepared to engage your banker in a discussion if necessary. I suggest that you also do a comparison of your income statements to previous months, quarters, and YTD. It is important to remember that net income is not cash, it is only the theory of cash because once again the P&L does not account for debt payments, owner draws, or disbursements, which are a use of cash.

Balance Sheet

A balance sheet is a snapshot in time and a record of the things you own and what you owe. On the left side is a record of everything you own such as cash, accounts receivables, inventory, plant, and equipment. On the right side in the upper section are the things you actually own, and in the bottom right section are the things you owe money on, or liabilities, both short term and long term. The right side of the balance sheet—the things you own plus what you owe—should balance with the left side (hence the reason it is called a balance sheet). Having an accurate balance sheet is vital to your business because it allows you to measure profitability. Understand that the balance sheet is a snapshot in time on one particular date (for example, December 31, 2018). I would suggest that you also use the balance sheet as a comparison tool. What does the balance sheet look like on December 31, 2018, compared to the same day in 2017 and 2016? Using the tool as a comparison helps you to see how your business is performing year to year.

I have run into a number of businesses using cash-based accounting principles. It is important to note that if you are using cash-based accounting, which I do not recommend, your accounts receivables and inventory will not show on your balance sheet. This can make a significant difference in the wealth within your business and your financial statements.

Your banker will consult your balance sheet to see your retained earnings in the business. The retained earnings are where wealth is created in your business. A common error that business owners fall into is taking too much revenue out of the business rather than building wealth. When you do this, you are making your business a greater risk for the bank. The greater the retained earnings in the business, the less the risk there is for the bank. Banks do not loan strictly from the P&L; they also look to the balance sheet.

Cash Flow

Cash is the lifeblood of your business and understanding how cash moves in and out of your business is critical. Will your daily operations generate enough cash to keep the business running and repay debt? For new and small businesses, cash flow is one of the most important issues.

Business owners often think of net income as cash, but, as we have discussed, net income at the bottom of your P&L or income statement is not cash but the theory of cash. The P&L does not take into account your debt (principal) payments and owner's draws on the business. Owners can be lured into thinking they are in a good cash position when in fact they are out of cash after paying debt and taking draws. Producing a cash flow projection helps to reveal what is really going on. Remember that account receivables are not cash; many businesses have gone out of business with account receivables on their books.

Because cash is so critical to staying in business, it always surprises me how few business owners produce cash flow projections. I had a client who was making money according to his net income line on the P&L, and he did not understand why he had no cash in the bank. Once we produced a cash flow projection, he could see how much he was spending to service debt and how his owner's draws were affecting cash in his business.

There are only four ways to get cash in your business:

1. Cash from sales
2. Cash from borrowing
3. Cash from investment
4. Cash from sales of assets

The best way to sustain your business is to generate cash from sales because eventually you will run out of both investment cash and your ability to borrow more cash. Furthermore, cash from borrowing and sometimes from investment will create a debt on your balance sheet, and the repayment of the interest and principal on the loan or investment is a use of cash that will reduce your available cash for operations.

Here are some ways to improve your cash flow:

1. Raise your prices.
2. Sell more.
3. Invoice immediately for work performed or services rendered, reducing days to cash.
4. Collect your receivables at a quicker pace.
5. Get longer terms with your vendors.
6. Reduce expenses.

A note on inventory: While inventory is an asset on your balance sheet, it is also a use of cash since you have most likely already paid for it. The unsold inventory sitting in your warehouse or on your shelf has your cash tied up and that cash is unavailable for you to use for day-to-day expenses. Excess inventory can be a huge drag on your business and your cash. The numbers drive everything in your business, and understanding those numbers—especially cash flow— helps you ask better questions in order to make better decisions. 💲

UNDERSTAND CREDIT

If you are planning on borrowing money from your local bank, you should go into it with a full understanding of the principles of credit. Bankers need to gauge your creditworthiness and they look at a number of things—in addition to your financials. These are often referred to as the five C's of credit. Let us take a look at each of them.

Character

How is your banker going to know and understand your character if you have not taken steps to establish a professional relationship with him or her? What if you have never even met your banker? Relationships take time and waiting until the time you need to borrow money is too late. Bankers want to minimize the risk of default and if they do not know you or have a long-term relationship with you, you are considered to be more of a risk. Some lenders consider your character as the most important decision-maker for them. Your character involves your prior business experience within the industry, your credit history, referrals, and references as well as your standing within your community.

Bankers will want to review your personal and business credit history before loaning you any money. It would be good for you to take the time to review your personal and business credit history before approaching the bank to ensure that there are no inaccuracies. If there are inaccuracies, get them corrected before going to see your banker.

Capacity

Do you have the capacity to repay the loan? Banks and bankers obviously want the money they loan to be repaid—and they want to see that you have the capacity to do so. If your debt-to-equity ratio is too high, your capacity to repay the debt is too low and it is unlikely you will get a loan. It is important for you to understand this ratio, not only on an ongoing basis as you run your business but also before you engage your banker to borrow additional funds. Bankers tend to loan at a 2:1 ratio, meaning they will loan two dollars for every one dollar of equity in the business, depending on your credit worthiness.

Capital

What kind of capital are you willing to put toward securing your loan? Any contribution by you the borrower helps to reduce the risk of default. Do you have personal wealth or assets that can be used as a secondary repayment source through the sale of the pledged asset? That is not much different than being required to put down 20 percent on a new home you are buying. The down payment on your home indicates how serious you are, which makes the lender more comfortable and more willing to make the loan.

Collateral

Do you have both business and personal collateral invested in your business? In other words, do you have skin in the game? Are you maxed out and leveraged to the hilt or do you have room to borrow additional funds? How good are your accounts receivables? How much cash do you have? What is the status of your inventory and hard assets within the business? These are questions you should be able to answer.

Conditions

What are the current conditions in the economy and your industry? What are the current trends and are they trending in your favor? Or is government regulation or other issues out of your control going to affect the business's ability to repay the loan? Who is your competition? Have you analyzed your competition's strengths and their weaknesses? How will you differentiate your business from the competition? Having an understanding of the conditions within your industry and the economy as well as being able to discuss these with your banker will give him or her confidence in your ability to manage your business. Conditions can also refer to how you, the borrower, intend to use the funds.

Aside from these five C's of creditworthiness, another major factor is trust. All relationships are built on trust—including banking relationships! Bankers have to trust that you have supplied current and accurate financial information. They have to trust that you have been truthful in how you have described your business, its current state and the desired future. Bankers want to know that you have a plan on how you are going to utilize the funds being borrowed and how you will pay them back. By consistently doing what you say you are going to do, you can build trust.

The bankers I interviewed want their customers to have a deep understanding of their financials as well as an understanding of debt and what that means for the business. They do not want to lend to business owners who are flying by the seat of their pants.

Your banker wants to know that you not only have the necessary experience but that you know what you are doing and take business seriously. $

COMMUNICATE PROACTIVELY

According to the bankers I spoke with, regular communication is paramount, and their best customers do this consistently. In fact, *proactive* communication is high on the list of what the bankers' best customers do well. It is also exactly what their poorly performing customers do not do well. Those customers often do not communicate at all unless, it is requested by the bank.

Regular communication is critical to a successful relationship with your banker. You want to be able to have honest conversations with your banker about what is going well and what is not going well; you should also share your plan to correct what is not going well. Set up regular meetings with your banker. Invite them to lunch or coffee, or offer to meet at their office to provide an update. I would suggest you do this at least once a quarter. It is also a good idea to invite your banker out to your offices or production facility to gain a deeper understanding of what you do.

You may find it easier to establish regular communication with your banker when times are good, but it is even more important to do so when times are not so good. Too often business owners hunker down and are afraid to deliver bad news to their banker. However, this is exactly the time you need to step up your game and deliver the bad news. Always go to the meeting with your banker prepared with a plan of action on how you will correct the situation. Bankers understand business and that all business has its ups and downs. According to one banker I spoke with, "Bankers take bad news well, and they take no news badly." Communicating during good and bad times keeps the doors open for your banker to be a trusted advisor and help you when times are tough. I would encourage you to develop a pattern of regular proactive communication with your banker. It will pay huge dividends.

I recommend asking your banker what they need from you and then making a point of executing on their wishes. Remember, they are there to help you, not to make your life miserable—but they have requirements they must adhere to. Listen to their request; arguing about it will undermine your partnership. They will do what they say they will do and so should you. Your banker's reputation with their bank is important, and it partially depends on your success. Provide your banker with all the information they are interested in, in a timely manner.

One of the best ways to keep your banker happy is to stay in compliance with the loan covenants that you agreed to when you borrowed money. These covenants protect the bank and ensure that they get their money back. As long as you stay in compliance, you should be on the path to make your banker happy.

Respect and good communication skills are important building blocks in your relationship; think of these things as another way to ensure the success of your business. Make sure that your communication is clear and concise. Your banker is busy and does not have time to read between the lines. Also, consider their workday. Do not call at 4 p.m. for a major transaction that needs to be done right away. The odds are that you knew about this need for a while, so why not be proactive and inform your banker so they can plan ahead for this request? Remember that your banker wants to provide excellent customer service to you, but you are not their only client. Proactive communication helps them to do the best job for you. If there is a wire transfer cutoff at 1:00 p.m., do not call at 12:30 to request the transfer. Inform your banker the day before you have this need.

This level of communication builds relationships. When your banker sees that you are invested in telling the truth and respect their time, their trust will grow. Put yourself in your banker's shoes and communicate the way you would want to be communicated with. This will produce great results for you. $

USE GOOD BUSINESS PRACTICES

Bankers like to see good business practices. As a business owner, you need a vision of where you are going and a plan on how you are going to get there. Bankers do not like businesses without a vision, direction, and a plan. A business owner who is shooting from the hip and hoping to get lucky does not interest bankers.

All successful businesses have a plan; that is why they are successful. Providing a thorough business plan and accurate forecasting (no pie in the sky here) with realistic numbers is the foundation for your good relationship with your banker. In addition, let your banker know what is unique about your company and how your loan request will further your competitive advantage. What is the value proposition you are offering your customers/clients? I also suggest that you create a realistic budget and compare actual results to the budget on a regular basis.

Bankers like to work with businesses that have documented policies and procedures on how work gets done; creating standard work and generating consistency of operations. This is what your banker really wants to see you aspire to. The larger the organization the more important these business practices are. What got you started in your business will often not get you to the next level; improvement and growth requires more advanced skill sets and more detailed planning. If you do not have these skill sets, you need to make the time to learn them. Get a business mentor, coach, or consultant to help you gain the valuable skills necessary to own, manage, and sustain a successful business. Do not leave your business success to chance.

A number of bankers reported seeing many businesses running by the seat of their pants. Those businesses have no business best practices in place to create standard operating procedures on how work gets done, and as a result they have inconsistencies in operations. Bankers know that a well-run company with good processes and procedures will help the business generate a greater profit margin, thereby reducing their risk. They know what to look for when looking at your company.

Documented processes and procedures may seem unnecessary but nothing could be further from the truth. This is a critical element to your success. Documented processes and procedures of reoccurring tasks will create standard work, which creates consistency of operations. Furthermore, these documented processes and procedures allow just about anyone to come into your business in a new position and get up to speed quickly. They also ensure that if you are not present at your business, it can still run effectively. Even better, your business has the potential to be worth more money if your operations are well documented. 💲

ENGAGE ADVISORS

You cannot do it alone. While you are starting out; you likely cannot afford to hire a management team, but there is no reason you cannot assemble a team of professionals to advise you when you need them. Once you are established and are generating revenue, you can consider putting a management team in place.

Take a look at the outline for any business plan. It will have a section for the executive team that will help you run your business. This is where you list the experience of your team that will help you to make the business a success.

If you are just starting out, create a list of professionals that you can turn to for guidance and advice. Your list might look like this:

- Banker
- Attorney
- Bookkeeper and/or accountant
- Insurance agent
- Business mentor or consultant

Take an honest assessment of the situation. Are you and your management team on the same page? Are you all headed in the same direction? If you have a clear vision and a plan on how you will bridge the gap between your current state and your desired future and your management team can articulate this, it will give your banker confidence. When the management team has training and vision, your banker's confidence will be greater because they know that kind of management team delivers results. Furthermore, a competent management team with breadth, depth, strength, and longevity prevents the operation from being fully dependent on the owner. All of these individuals you are depending on to help you obtain and sustain success should become your trusted advisors. Be proactive and intentional to get the advice and guidance you need. $

DEMONSTRATE PROFESSIONALISM

Your banker is a professional, and you always want to present yourself as no less professional than your banker. This does not mean that you need to wear a suit and tie when meeting, but it does mean that you need to be prepared. Documents need to be accurate, neat, and organized without spelling errors and coffee stains. It may require you to step up your game a little. Meeting your banker is not like meeting your friends at the local pub. Your banker is a professional and you should dress and act professionally. Your demeanor is also important, you want to come across as confident but not cocky. Remember that you are representing your personal business brand. How do you want to be perceived? In all relationships, perception matters. Run everything you might present to your banker (documents, email, your website, and yourself) through the lens of your banker's eye before you send something to them or meet.

Show competence by being prepared with accurate documents as well as knowledge about your industry and your business. Be polite and treat your banker with the same level of respect you would treat your very best customer, and always, always be on time. Being reliable shows respect. When communicating through written correspondence with your banker, make sure that you are brief and to the point. This also applies to phone conversations. Most important is to be accountable. If you make a mistake, admit that you did, take ownership, and explain what happened and how you plan to correct it. This is the level of professionalism that will help to establish a trusting relationship with your banker. $

FOCUS ON THE CUSTOMER

Bankers know that for your business to succeed, it must be customer focused. The customer or client is the whole reason you are in business. It is the foundation of strategy to determine how to meet the customers' need or solve their problem, then organize your company in such a way to do so in the most effective and efficient manner. How are you going to meet your customers' needs? Is your business organized to meet those needs effectively and efficiently? Is your management team focused on meeting customer needs? What about your employees?

Are you able to explain to your banker how you are meeting your customers' need? What pain or problem are you solving for your customer? Strategy is an intentional focus and alignment of resources that deliver maximum results for the customer. Before your company can organize to meet a customer's need or eliminate a pain or problem, you need to fully understand what that pain or problem is.

Your bankers are well versed in business. They will be able to recognize what you are attempting to accomplish in this area. Explaining all of this to your banker helps them to understand how you are focused on the customer. Your job as a business owner is to understand the customer in such a way that you can exceed their expectations in solving their problem or achieving their goals. Be able to explain to your banker who your customers are, what product or service you are providing to meet or exceed their needs, and where they are located geographically. How is your company organized to meet those needs and provide superior performance? Presenting this information will help inspire your banker's confidence. $

EXPRESS APPRECIATION

Bankers, more so than ever before, especially since the great downturn, are interested in building relationships with their clients. They are not much different than you the business owner who understands that your business is about people and the relationship you have with your customers and clients.

Your banker is an important partner in your business and should be treated as such. One of the best strategies you can have for your business is to have a great working relationship with your banker, and that takes effort on your part. It may be necessary to interview a number of banks and bankers in order to find the right fit for you, your business, and your industry. A banker that understands you and your industry, one who understands and is willing to support your organization, can be a genuine asset. It is your responsibility to treat this relationship with your banker as one that is not solely about the money right now. By investing in a long-term relationship with your banker, you are investing in the long-term health of your business.

The more that your banker understands you and your business the lower the risk is for him or her. Having an excellent relationship with your banker also means you are not switching banks for a quarter or half basis point. You are putting value on the relationship and not just the finance charges and interest rates. Think of your ideal customer or client. Do you want them switching vendors over a few cents or dollars after you have worked hard to build a great relationship? I think not. Bankers are no different.

I do not want to discredit the big banks, but after working with small to mid-market companies for many years, I prefer the small to mid-market banks. I have found that with the big banks it is difficult to get to know your banker because they seem to churn through people. You can establish a relationship with your local branch and return a few months later and find that the individual you were working with has moved on; now you have start over educating the new banker. All of the bankers I interviewed have been with their small to mid-market branch for many years, creating lasting relationships with their customers. They are usually involved in the local community in some way and often attend local networking events. This is the kind of banker you are looking for. $

BE PROACTIVE

It concerns bankers when they see business owners being reactive rather than proactive with running the business. The business owner who does not have a plan or is not following the plan is a potential risk for the bank. Being reactive is when you react to everything that comes your way. Vision and a detailed plans are the guardrails that prevent you from getting lost in being reactive. That is why bankers want to see this kind of planning. They want to know that your actions are being guided by something more lasting than the day-to-day issues and problems that crop up.

Being able to explain to your banker how you will execute on your plan is important. This gives them greater confidence that you will achieve your goals and continue to grow as a company—because all great companies have plans. Having a well-run business with a clear strategy and vision along with goals and an action plan that will help you achieve the results you are looking is being proactive. Too many times business owners wait for a crisis to provoke change, but this is being reactive and it does not lead to great results. Do not wait for a crisis; instead, create a vision for the future, set goals, and make a plan of action. Demonstrating this approach in your business gives your banker confidence that you are proactive and will be able to achieve the results you are targeting.

Of course, business does not always go as we plan, but if you are proactive, you are solution focused. Proactive people take responsibility for what is happening and then come up with a plan to correct the situation. Furthermore, your vision and goals help to mitigate the negative impact of unfortunate business developments; they also keep you on track during difficult times. The first habit in *The Seven Habits of Highly Effective People* by Stephen Covey is "Be Proactive." I recommend that you read it for yourself and apply its lessons to your business—and to your relationship with your banker. $

DEVELOP SUCCESSION PLANS

Since so many baby boomers are now in a position to sell their businesses or transition them, I was curious about what the bankers would report regarding how many of their customers had succession plans in place. Most bankers reported that not enough had succession plans in place; but as you might expect, they also reported that the best-run companies were addressing this issue.

A succession plan does not mean that you are planning on selling your business right away. It does mean that you are planning for the future of your business should something happen to you prematurely. If you are thinking of selling or exiting your business, you should start preparing at least three years in advance. The sales or transition process takes time—more time than most business owners realize.

One of the major upsides to thinking and planning for succession is that it forces you to take a hard look at your business. What is going well and what is not going well? What needs improvement? Is your business organized for success? Would someone be interested in buying your business in its current state? Is the business generating sufficient revenue and profits? Are you building wealth in the business or avoiding taxes?

When it comes to succession planning, I suggest that you focus on the management side first (as opposed to the ownership side). Without adequate management in place, ownership will not be able to have a smooth transition of the business internally or externally.

Without a succession plan in place your business and your personal wealth is at risk. If something tragic should happen to ownership the business is in jeopardy of failing. Good succession planning is a bit like insurance. It has great benefit later, but it also has benefits now in the planning process itself. It also pays off in your relationship with your banker, boosting their confidence in your business. $

THE NOT SO GOOD, THE BAD, AND THE UGLY

In addition to the ten keys to making your banker happy, the bankers I interviewed offered some insight into the issues that give them pause. Consider these pointers as things you should avoid if you want to cultivate a good relationship with your banker.

Hubris

Sometimes business owners think they can handle issues without getting any help or guidance, or they choose not to take their banker's advice. Sometimes pride and ego get in the way of common sense. Any sign of arrogance or hubris on your part is a red flag to your banker. Do not let your ego get in the way of your success. Remember: Your banker is there to help you. He or she wants you to be successful, but you have to be open to input and guidance. Your ego needs to be checked at the door if you want to be successful.

I have run into a number of business owners whose ego has gotten in the way of listening to not only their banker but also consultants and other advisers trying to help them. They think they can do it themselves, but if that were the case, they would have already done so and they would not be in their current predicament.

Success requires advice and guidance. Not only do you risk your relationship with your banker if you choose not to listen, you risk the ongoing success of your business. Rarely is anything of great significance accomplished alone; it always takes the help of others.

Business owners often are so caught up in the day-to-day of their businesses that they cannot see what is really going on. Input from another source, one without emotional involvement, is invaluable. Sometimes those on the outside can see more clearly. There is no need to let ego or hubris get in the way of seeking help. Just think of professional athletes who are at the top of their game. They still have multiple coaches to help them get better. They do not settle for the status quo, and neither should you.

Dishonesty

When bankers were discussing customers whose businesses are not performing well, the issue of dishonesty came up. Unfortunately, some business owners intentionally provide inaccurate financial statements to try to make their business look like it is doing better than it is. This will kill your relationship and trust level with your banker and the bank. There is no room for dishonesty in any of your business dealings, including with your banker. Integrity is paramount if you want to have a long-term relationship with your banker.

Lack of Understanding About Risk

Risk is a big issue with bankers. They want their customers to understand the risks of their investment decisions, and they want owners to discuss their plans with the bank before acting on those plans when it affects the bank's interest. Taking unnecessary risk will create concern for your banker. They are there to help you manage the risk and not endanger their investment in you and your business.

It is a banker's job to understand risk; my advice is to listen to them. Of course, a well thought out, comprehensive business plan, good values, clear direction, and goals will all help to reduce risk as well. Staying in compliance with your covenants and the necessary laws will also reduce risk. Paying attention to your financials on an ongoing basis goes a long way to reduce risk. Learning to maximize value will help to minimize risk for you and your banker. As a business owner, you should be well versed in risk management.

Taking Too Much Out of the Business

This is a common problem with business owners who are trying to avoid paying taxes or those who do not understand cash flow. A few bankers mentioned that some business owners take too much out of their business in the form of owner's draws or dividends, putting the business at risk should things not turn out as planned. In that case, the owners need to come back to the bank to borrow additional funds. Bankers are concerned about business owners who are taking too much profit out of the business and are not building wealth and retained earnings. Remember that bankers look at retained earnings on your balance sheet to determine your ability to borrow.

According to the bankers, allowing for taxes at 30 to 40 percent and then a little more for lifestyle and return on capital to the owner is good business practice. It is important to communicate with your banker what this target percentage is. When dividends exceed 100 percent of profits, there is a lot of explaining required.

It is also imperative that you do not chronically overdraw your deposit accounts. Rare instances are okay and bankers understand them—especially if there is an email from you saying you are sorry and that you made a mistake. But if this happens more than two to three times a year, it suggests that your internal controls are not adequate, and that will add strain to your relationship with your banker.

Bankers are notified first thing in the morning each time one of their customer's accounts is overdrawn. These issues have a high degree of visibility since they are technically short-term extensions of unsecured credit. Then they have to spend a portion of their morning reaching out to you to figure out when a deposit or transfer will be made to cover the NSF items; this is a surefire way to kill goodwill at the bank. $

MAKE YOUR BANKER HAPPY

Bankers are looking for:

1. Businesses that know and understand their financials
2. Business owners that proactively communicate with the bank
3. Businesses that have good business practices and documented processes and procedures in place
4. Businesses with a seasoned management team in place or access to those who can advise them
5. Businesses that have organized their operations to maximize effectiveness and efficiency
6. Business owners who take their relationship with the bank seriously and act in a professional and ethical manner
7. Businesses that are focused on meeting customer needs
8. Owners that want to have a long-term relationship with their bank
9. Business owners who are proactive, not reactive
10. Business owners who understand that having succession plans in place will reduce risk for not only the owners and employees but also the bank

11. Businesses that avoid the not so good, the bad, and the ugly like the plague

Your banker wants to help you succeed and that requires good business practices on your part. The better you get in these key areas, the more confident your banker will be that your business will be able to weather the storms that come your way.

I know a number of bankers serving small to mid-market companies, more than I interviewed here. These bankers are normal people who care deeply about what they do and about their customers. They love to see their customers doing well, and they truly enjoy working with their customers. It is why they are in business. They particularly like working with customers who appreciate the trusted advisor relationship. Finding the right bank with the right banker should be on top of your priority list. If you already have a banker, getting to know him or her and building a trusted relationship is critical to your success. Think of it like dating. You meet your banker and learn more about them and they learn more about you. Being honest is the most important aspect of establishing a long-term relationship. In order for the relationship to go further, it takes effort on your part and that takes continual and effective communication. Trust is not built in one meeting; it takes consistent effort on your part. In short, be proactive and intentional about creating a long and lasting relationship with your banker. Follow these bankers' advice and you will be on your way to a relationship that will serve you and your business well. The benefits of doing so will pay returns for many years to come.

Gary Furr, MBA, is an experienced CEO, COO, and internationally sought-after consultant. He is in the business of helping business owners make more money, reducing the risk for their bank and banker. Gary's approach has grown out of forty-plus years of C-Level business experience, an MBA in organizational development, and countless interactions with business owners, observing their struggles to achieve the level of success that they envisioned when they started their business. For the last several years, Gary has helped business owners and executives improve productivity, increase capacity and reduce waste in their businesses and has successfully increased bottom-line revenues in some cases by more than 1000 percent.

I interact with a group of bankers on a regular basis. If you are in need of a small to mid-market bank, I can guide you. And, if you are struggling in your business or want to take your business to another level, I can help you achieve dramatic results.

www.garyfurrconsulting.com / 503-312-3145

If you are looking for more tried-and-true business advice in book form, take a look at another book I wrote just for that purpose: *It's Not Hard, It's Business.* $

Made in the USA
Las Vegas, NV
13 September 2022

55179545R00026